LOVE IS A

SAUSAGE

DOG

summersdale

LOVE IS A SAUSAGE DOG

Copyright © Summersdale Publishers Ltd, 2017

Images © Shutterstock.com and Darren Triggs

An Hachette UK Company
www.hachette.co.uk

Summersdale Publishers Ltd
Part of Octopus Publishing Group Limited
Carmelite House
50 Victoria Embankment
LONDON
EC4Y 0DZ
UK

www.summersdale.com

Printed and bound in the Czech Republic

ISBN: 978-1-84953-987-6

Substantial discounts on bulk quantities of Summersdale books are available to corporations, professional associations and other organisations. For details contact general enquiries: telephone: +44 (0) 1243 771107 or email: enquiries@summersdale.com.

INTRODUCTION

Anything a dog can do, a dachshund can do better… whether that be tunnelling through blankets or staging acrobatic displays over molehills. These pint-sized pooches are loyal to the core, and with their loveable waddle and eyes that would melt even a tiger's heart, who wouldn't fall for their charm? Always ready to provide comfort, companionship and joy, dachshunds truly are our tiny best friends.

♥ SAUSAGE DOGS ♥

FOR THE WIN

THE DACHSHUND IS A PERFECTLY
ENGINEERED DOG. IT IS PRECISELY
LONG ENOUGH FOR A SINGLE
STANDARD STROKE OF THE BACK,
BUT YOU AREN'T PAYING FOR
ANY SUPERFLUOUS LEG.

Mary Doria Russell

ALL YOU NEED IS LOVE...

♥ AND A ♥

DACHSHUND

BUY A PUP AND YOUR MONEY WILL BUY LOVE UNFLINCHING THAT CANNOT LIE.

Rudyard Kipling

SAUSAGE DOGS

— TINY, SASSY AND

HEART-MELTINGLY

♥ ADORABLE ♥

A DOG TEACHES A BOY
FIDELITY, PERSEVERANCE,
AND TO TURN AROUND
THREE TIMES BEFORE
LYING DOWN.

Robert Benchley

TO BOLDLY GO

WHERE NO

DACHSHUND

HAS GONE BEFORE

THE MORE I SEE OF THE REPRESENTATIVES OF THE PEOPLE, THE MORE I ADMIRE MY DOGS.

Alphonse de Lamartine

LOOK DEEP INTO
MY EYES... YOU FEEL
❤ COMPELLED TO ❤

BUY ME A BONE

THEY NEVER TALK ABOUT
THEMSELVES BUT LISTEN TO
YOU WHILE YOU TALK ABOUT
YOURSELF, AND KEEP UP AN
APPEARANCE OF BEING INTERESTED
IN THE CONVERSATION.

Jerome K. Jerome

WARNING:
DO NOT STEP
♥ ON THE ♥

GUARD DOG

EVERYTHING I KNOW, I LEARNED FROM DOGS.

Nora Roberts

♥ SOME THINGS JUST ♥

FILL YOUR HEART

WITHOUT TRYING

THE SECRET OF ARCHITECTURAL EXCELLENCE IS TO TRANSLATE THE PROPORTIONS OF A DACHSHUND INTO BRICKS, MORTAR AND MARBLE.

Christopher Wren

ENJOY

 THE

LITTLE THINGS

DACHSHUNDS ARE REALLY PEOPLE WITH SHORT LEGS IN FUR COATS.

Anonymous

BODY OF A SAUSAGE,
BRAINS OF A FOX,
HEART OF A LION

WHOEVER SAID YOU CAN'T BUY HAPPINESS FORGOT LITTLE PUPPIES.

Gene Hill

IT'S ALWAYS A GOOD DAY

♥ TO BE A ♥

SAUSAGE DOG

DOGS ARE MIRACLES WITH PAWS.

Susan Ariel Rainbow Kennedy

THE JOURNEY OF LIFE
IS SWEETER
WHEN TRAVELLED
♥ WITH A ♥

DACHSHUND

NO ONE APPRECIATES THE VERY SPECIAL GENIUS OF YOUR CONVERSATION AS THE DOG DOES.

Christopher Morley

SILENCE IS GOLDEN,
UNLESS YOU HAVE A

DACHSHUND

— THEN IT'S JUST
♥ SUSPICIOUS ♥

DACHSHUND:
A HALF-A-DOG HIGH AND A DOG-AND-A-HALF LONG.

H. L. Mencken

WHOEVER SAID
DIAMONDS ARE A
GIRL'S BEST FRIEND
♥ NEVER HAD A ♥
_____

DACHSHUND
_____

A DOG IS THE ONLY THING ON EARTH THAT LOVES YOU MORE THAN HE LOVES HIMSELF.

Josh Billings

LIFE IS BETTER

♥ WITH A ♥

DACHSHUND

DOGS LAUGH,
BUT THEY LAUGH
WITH THEIR TAILS.

Max Eastman

DACHSHUNDS

♥ ARE NOT ♥
OUR WHOLE LIFE,
BUT THEY MAKE OUR
LIVES WHOLE

THOUGH SHE BE BUT LITTLE, SHE IS FIERCE.

William Shakespeare

HOME

♥ IS ♥

WHERE YOUR
DACHSHUND IS

YOU ARE YOU BECAUSE YOUR LITTLE DOG KNOWS YOU.

Gertrude Stein

FIRST WE STEAL YOUR ♥ HEART, ♥ AND THEN WE

STEAL YOUR BED

IF YOU ARE A DOG AND
YOUR OWNER SUGGESTS
THAT YOU WEAR A
SWEATER... SUGGEST
THAT HE WEAR A TAIL.

Fran Lebowitz

I DON'T OWN MY
♥ DACHSHUND, ♥
MY DACHSHUND

OWNS ME

FROM THE DOG'S POINT
OF VIEW, HIS MASTER
IS AN ELONGATED AND
ABNORMALLY CUNNING DOG.

Mabel Louise Robinson

DID SOMEONE ♥ SAY ♥

SLINKY?

NOTHING WILL TURN A MAN'S HOME INTO A CASTLE MORE QUICKLY AND EFFECTIVELY THAN A DACHSHUND.

Queen Victoria

I LOVE YOU MORE THAN ANYTHING...

♥ EXCEPT MY ♥

DACHSHUND

MY LITTLE DOG
— A HEARTBEAT
AT MY FEET.

Edith Wharton

BEST FRIENDS

COME IN ALL DIFFERENT
SHAPES AND SIZES...
ONLY THE BEST COME
WITH SHORT LEGS AND
♥ LONG TORSOS ♥

IF IT WASN'T FOR DOGS, SOME PEOPLE WOULD NEVER GO FOR A WALK.

Emily Dickinson

I LIVE IN A MADHOUSE

♥ WITH A ♥

TINY ARMY

THAT I CREATED MYSELF

I'VE SEEN A LOOK IN DOGS' EYES, A QUICKLY VANISHING LOOK OF AMAZED CONTEMPT, AND I AM CONVINCED THAT BASICALLY DOGS THINK HUMANS ARE NUTS.

John Steinbeck

KEEP CALM
AND
♥ LOVE A ♥
DACHSHUND

WHY DO DACHSHUNDS WEAR THEIR EARS INSIDE OUT?

P. G. Wodehouse

If you're interested in finding out more about our books, find us on Facebook at **Summersdale Publishers** and follow us on Twitter at **@Summersdale**.

www.summersdale.com